THE MAGGI PLAN

A Simple & Easy Retirement Solution

ROBERT MAGGI & CHRIS MAGGI

D1247611

Printed in the United States of America

First Printing, 2019

Gradient Positioning Systems, LLC
4105 Lexington Avenue North, Suite 110
Arden Hills, MN 55126
(877) 901-0894

Contributors: Gradient Positioning Systems, LLC.

TABLE OF CONTENTS

INTRODUCTION

Retirement planning is personal. It affects you and your spouse, and often members of your immediate and extended family. It is a process that can seem intimidating and uncomfortable. Going to a large, impersonal corporation to get cookie-cutter advice can dissuade even the most responsible individuals from adequately preparing for a big part of their life. You're looking for insights and knowledge from a seasoned professional. Feeling like the advice and options presented to you have *you* in mind is essential. Bobby and Chris Maggi agree. They're a father and son team that specializes in comprehensive retirement planning with a commitment to treating you like family.

Approaching three decades of experience, Bobby began his career by helping clients navigate the ins and outs of Medicare and long-term health insurance. As the business progressed, it was evident that people needed help with other aspects of retirement. Eager to follow in his father's footsteps, Chris got a jumpstart on his career in high school. While most of his high school peers aspired to get their driver's licenses, Chris held an insurance license! After majoring in finance and minoring in accounting in college, Chris originally planned for a job on Wall Street. But soon, he realized his passion lay in helping people with more than just one aspect of their financial lives. He decided to team up with his father to combine their separate but complementary skill sets to educate clients and develop complete plans to navigate the road to and through retirement.

Today, that road has more twists and turns than ever. In years past, retirement planning was more straightforward. For example, your parents may have had a pension from a company that employed them for their entire career. They probably had some money saved, as well, and had Social Security and Medicare to fall back on. It's not so simple anymore. Instead of one job, it's two, three, or maybe more per spouse, each with an individual 401(k). Markets are more volatile with significant corrections that leave you feeling like your future is hanging in the balance. Healthcare and taxes haven't got any less complex, either. A financial planner trying to sell you a particular product their company is pushing doesn't account for all of this complexity.

You probably have questions—questions that cover more than just a single investment product. Questions like:

- Will I have enough money for retirement?
- How can I get more growth out of my investments?
- Am I paying too much in taxes and fees?
- How do I account for long-term care, if needed?

These are things they don't teach in high school, or even college!

And those are just the questions you can think of off the top of your head. Meeting with a professional who can look at the big picture is critical. Otherwise, you don't know what you don't know! That can lead to mistakes. Bobby and Chris routinely meet with prospective clients who are unwittingly making mistakes that can be costly in the long run. Some of the most common are:

- Not adequately protecting your assets
- No beneficiary planning
- No powers of attorney
- Ignoring investments/financial statements
- Putting off planning for retirement or believing it's too late to start planning

Think of it like building a house. Would you hire an electrician only? Do they draw up blueprints? Install plumbing? Pour the foundation? A home with the best wiring doesn't mean much when it doesn't have a roof! You need someone who can help you account for and deal with every aspect of your retirement. You need a plan. A COMPLETE plan. You need the MAGGI PLAN. Born of this father and son partnership, the Maggi Plan addresses your unique set of circumstances. Including your income, Social Security benefit, insurance, investments, and estate and tax planning.

Hosts of both a weekly radio and TV show, Bobby and Chris are passionate about sharing their perspective on retirement and other financial matters. In addition to their weekly media appearances, they also specialize in helping employees of the federal government get the most out of their unique set of benefits, including Federal Employee Group Life Insurance (FEGLI). Federal employees can learn more at www.federaleducators.com. This book is meant to be an additional resource as you educate yourself on the various topics involved with retirement. In the coming chapters, we will touch on multiple methods and issues that can help you prepare a complete plan so you can enjoy your retirement to the fullest.

1
CHOOSING A FINANCIAL SERVICES PROVIDER/ ARCHITECT

As we discussed previously, developing a retirement strategy can seem daunting. With so much at stake, you must partner with someone who makes you comfortable. We don't just want to work with individuals who need financial planning. We work with individuals who *want* to work with us. To be successful, you and your financial planner must have a shared philosophy and the same goals in mind. Most people can tell the difference between a salesperson and a professional who stresses strategies and processes. They make things simple and emphasize education instead of sales pitches.

Here are some key things to consider when choosing your financial services provider:
- How do you charge for your services?
- What licenses, credentials, or other certifications do you have?
- What services do you or your firm provide?
- Can you provide me with a sample plan?
- What is your investment approach?
- How much contact do you have with your clients?
- Do clients work with you or a team?
- What makes your client experience unique?

Tax strategies are another subject to bring up. It is a critical aspect of retirement planning and is one of the first things we bring up when meeting with a client.

STARTING YOUR SEARCH

Like most things today, finding a financial services provider will probably begin by using the Internet. A simple online search should yield plenty of options in your area. Be sure to review company websites to get an idea of their approach and to get an idea about their qualifications and history. See if they're in the news. Is it good? Bad? Taking a look at their social media pages is a good idea as well. It can help give you an idea of their engagement with clients and give you a view of what things they find valuable.

Using technology in this way can also help you feel more comfortable about initially contacting prospective financial services providers. The buffer of websites and review boards can also give you time to formulate questions to ask. People can be on guard during an initial face-to-face meeting. You're usually in their office to start. While the chairs might be comfortable, and the setting pleasant, the thought of discussing the intricate details of your finances with someone you just met can be very off-putting.

Spending time online to do an initial search could be very beneficial and save you considerable time down the road.

If you're still not comfortable after doing some initial research online, asking for referrals might be a good next step. Personal recommendations can help you to focus your search efforts, as your family, friends, and colleagues know you best. People are usually eager to help with some friendly advice. Just keep in mind that the qualities they're looking for in a financial services provider might not be the ones you are looking for.

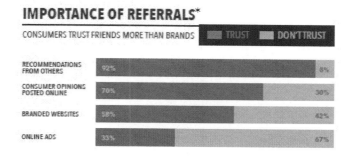

IMPORTANCE OF REFERRALS*

CONSUMERS TRUST FRIENDS MORE THAN BRANDS ░ TRUST ░ DON'T TRUST

RECOMMENDATIONS FROM OTHERS	92%	8%
CONSUMER OPINIONS POSTED ONLINE	70%	30%
BRANDED WEBSITES	58%	42%
ONLINE ADS	33%	67%

Research and referrals aren't a replacement for a face-to-face meeting, or a phone call. To truly get a feel for a specific financial services professional or firm, you'll need to connect personally. You should see if what you've been reading matches up with reality. This might sound obvious to baby boomers and other more mature generations who find that the online experience lacks the personal touch they're accustomed to. Face to face meetings and interpersonal relationships have been a routine part of your life. Making a decision this big isn't going to be done via email alone.

---

* *https://www.business2community.com/marketing/referral-marketing-matter-0944226*

FACE-TO-FACE

We strive to treat our clients like family. It's not just about "I" or "me", it's about you! When you meet in person with any financial services planner, you should feel comfortable. There shouldn't be a one-way conversation where all you do is give out fact after fact about your finances. Remember what interested you about them in the first place, and be sure to ask questions. They should have clear reasons for asking about specific information and provide context, so everything makes sense.

Now that you've asked your questions, did they have any questions for you besides general information or financial details? Did they seem interested in your situation or go on about themselves? Did they ask to see what your main retirement concerns are? This relationship is going to be ongoing, so you and your financial services provider should "click." Everything needs to feel right for this to be successful for both parties.

BIAS

We've all heard the term *bias* used frequently in other aspects of life. Media bias, political bias, it goes on and on. We all come to the table with our own experiences, backgrounds, preferences, and definitions of success. These can all affect how we look at retirement planning, and it is something you should be aware of as you interview prospective financial services providers. A true professional should be very open and honest about their entire career and background. It will give you a real sense of whether your philosophies and goals align. It can be a red flag if you can't get a good understanding of these things during an initial meeting. Is this just a job to them or an actual career? Are they only a transactional agent, or are they a fiduciary with your best interest at heart?

Bias can also limit what a given professional can advise you on. Depending on their qualifications, they may only cover on an aspect of retirement planning or be able to offer a particular set of products. Titles like CFP, CFA, and other acronyms can be a clue about what direction they may try to steer you in.

The company they work for can also be an obvious clue. For example, insurance companies like to sell insurance. So, if you go to them with questions, it's reasonable to expect most of their answers and solutions will be insurance-based. Even if it seems that they provide more general retirement planning services. That's why it's so important to work with a Registered Investor Advisory (RIA) firm, like ours! All kidding aside, no matter who you work with, this registration is valuable to look for. It means that they're not obligated to press products from a specific company. It is incumbent on them to make sure you have a complete plan that's made for your benefit.

Another vital thing to look for during your research is to see if your prospective financial services providers are held to the fiduciary standard. This standard dictates that any recommendation they make or product they offer has to be beneficial to you and your specific situation, even if that product or service is less favorable to them. In other words, they can't merely recommend something to make a quick sale.

Alternatively, there is a separate set of standards known as suitability standards. This standard leaves more wiggle room. Instead of being explicitly required to hold your interests above any other, this standard says that anything recommended to their clients should be expected to be suitable for that client's specific situation. It's a distinction with a big difference and is something you need to look for.

Another way to determine any bias in the decision making of a financial services provider is to find out how they charge for services. How much they charge can be a consideration, too, but how they charge can tell you more. If they're paid on commission like a car salesperson, it means that the more they sell, the more they make. That can consciously or subconsciously affect the products and services they recommend. Instead, find someone who is paid by fees for services. Basically, this means that your success is their success!

DIY

The work it takes to identify bias and find someone you trust might seem like a lot of trouble. You might even begin to think that maybe taking care of your retirement planning yourself might be more manageable. After all, we just said the Internet is a powerful research tool. Perhaps that's all you need. Before you decide to handle everything on your own, let's think back to the homebuilding analogy.

A small leak from the kitchen faucet doesn't seem like a big deal. You'll take care of it when you have a chance. You start by looking at different videos online, reading various how-to articles about fixing leaks, and reading multiple forums written by people in similar situations. But, you can't quite find the video or article that talks about your specific faucet. If you do find the right information, you notice that you need a particular tool to do a thorough and correct job. Now you have to buy that tool and find the parts all by yourself.

Meanwhile, water is also leaking in the wall behind your faucet, causing a lot of damage. How much money would you have saved, and how much stress would you have avoided, if you had called a plumber to fix that leak in the first place? The same holds for financial planning. Having professional help to do things right in the first place can save you lots of money and heartache in the long run.

Here are some trade-offs to consider when deciding to go it alone.

	D-I-Y	WORKING WITH A PROFESSIONAL
EFFORT	Significant: work done by self	Minimal: most work done on your behalf
COST	Lower cost compared with professional	Fees or commissions
ADVICE	Personal research required	Industry education, licenses and experience
TOOLS	Generic online sample tools	Access to valuable reports, secure document storage, etc.

If you're still thinking about doing your own retirement planning, please keep in mind that technology can be biased just like people. Think about it. The financial websites were probably created for a reason other than dispensing free advice. Often, the aim is to steer you towards a specific product. It could be one they offer, or a product another company is paying them to promote. They also might have the goal of getting some of your basic information. If you put income or age information into a financial calculator or take an online survey, you could get some useful information. The tradeoff is that the data you just divulged could be used to market additional products or services to you. This isn't to say these sites or tools are all nefarious. You just need to take this into consideration.

Remember, finding a financial services provider you want to work with is vital. They should help you with formulating a complete plan for your income, Social Security benefit, insurance, Medicare, investments, estate, and tax situation.

CHAPTER RECAP

- Use the Internet not only to study financial strategies but also to find a financial services provider.
- Check for bias—ensure they have your best interests at heart.
- Ask questions.
- Did they ask you questions?
- Does the relationship "click"?
- Before you do it yourself, be sure to consider everything that's involved.
- Working with a professional could alleviate a lot of headaches down the road.

2
TODAY'S RETIREMENT

YOYO! No, we don't mean the toy, and we don't mean YOLO (You Only Live Once). We mean that in securing your financial future, *you're on your own*. That might sound stark, but it's not! It's simply different. Retirement isn't as straightforward as it used to be. Pensions are a thing of the past, interest rates are persistently low, people are living longer than ever, and healthcare costs continue to rise. Let's touch on a few of these new realities.

Life expectancy is up, and that's a good thing! Americans, on average, live to almost 80 years of age. In 1960 it was closer to 70.* That's a testament to advancements in science and society, and it is something you need to take into account. It means you'll

---

* *https://www.cdc.gov/nchs/fastats/life-expectancy.htm*

probably need more money for retirement, but you'll also have more time to make money.

Over the last several years, interest rates have been persistently low. This fact has turned methods of growing your money that were once thought to be relatively safe into riskier investment strategies. If you're stashing money in savings accounts or bank CDs, you'll be sorry to hear that the interest accrued on these accounts are often not covering the rate of inflation. So, as the years go by, you are losing the value that you could have enjoyed if you would put your money into investments geared for more growth*.

While interest rates have stayed low, health insurance costs have skyrocketed. Whether it's anecdotes from friends, news stories, or from opening a bill with an eye-popping sum, the costs associated with healthcare are real and significant. For example, $7,698 represents the median monthly cost for a private room in a nursing home.**

Those are real challenges but think of it this way. Your success up to this point has been a direct result of your ability to overcome problems with hard work and education. This challenge will be another chapter in your story of success. Plus, new strategies and technologies have been developed to help you keep your goals within reach.

TECHNOLOGY

Today, you can harness the power of the Internet for almost limitless information. Desktops, laptops, tablets, smartphones, and more all bring you the latest news, theories, and offers about retirement. Email is a normal part of your professional life, and you're accustomed to paying bills and securing other services online. Paying the gas bill and hiring a gardener is one thing,

---

* http://www.businessinsider.com/chart-5000-years-of-interest-rates-history-2016-6
** http://www.modernhealthcare.com/article/20160510/news/160519999

but are you confident enough in your digital skills to risk your retirement on them?

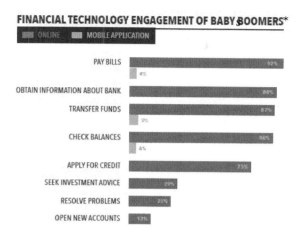

You have probably already done some research, and since you're reading this book, we imagine you might be suffering from information overload. With all the theories, strategies, and products that are available to you at the touch of a button, it can all seem overwhelming.

Financial services providers have access to a variety of automated tools and software. Be sure to ask about what sort of technology a prospective planner uses and see if they can demonstrate how it will be useful to you. Powerful tools can only be practical when made for the specific task at hand. They should educate and show you your options in an efficient manner. You need more than just charts and graphs about the past performance of the market to know what to do.

* http://www.nielsen.com/us/en/insights/news/2014/digital-money-management-millennials-and-boomers.html

We use maximization software that can take your specific circumstances into account and present you with scenarios based on different strategies. Besides telling you how much money you could make; it can help you determine how comfortable you are with one plan or another. Ultimately, using technology should help clarify the process and details of your finances. If it doesn't do that, then it's not useful.

EMPOWERING WOMEN

We already know that retirement today is drastically different than it used to be. With all that's involved in planning for the next stage in life, it's important to make sure everyone involved is on the same page. Women have unique challenges in retirement. With longer life expectancies, women need to ensure that they'll have enough income to meet their expenses. And if their spouse passes away before them, they need to ensure that any transferable benefits are handled correctly. It's also more likely for women to be the primary caregiver for children or other members of the family. This caregiving can cut down on the years they are able to work and plan for retirement.

Education is vital to ensure both husband and wife have input into their retirement. Both need to understand their assets and know what they are and how to access them. Your retirement plan will be that much stronger if all parties are involved and consulted.

CHAPTER RECAP

- Financial and societal changes have changed retirement planning.
- Ensure both you and your spouse are involved with the retirement process.
- Financial services providers can help you cut through the clutter and help you determine what information is relevant to you.
- Specialized tools like maximization software can help inform you on the best strategies.

3

ACCUMULATION AND DISTRIBUTION
"LAYING THE FOUNDATION AND MOVING IN"

Accumulation is like when you start building a house. Using the best tools and materials, you start with the foundation and move onto the frame. Slowly the house begins to take shape. The end product is income that will last, just like you a house that's built to stand the test of time. The roof shouldn't leak after a few rain showers, and the foundation shouldn't crumble under a little stress. When building wealth, you want to use modern techniques that help grow over your lifetime, despite the occasional market storm. You want those assets to be there for you when you're ready to retire.

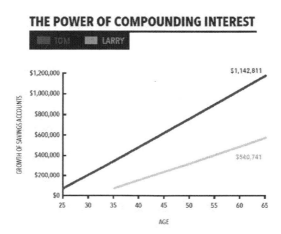

Like most things, the sooner you start saving for your retirement, the better. As you can see in the graphic above, waiting to begin funding your retirement by a few years early in your life can result in substantial differences. This graph is an example of two people who started with the same base amount of money but invested at different times. Retirement might mean something different to Larry than it does to Tom. But, we're pretty sure Larry would still like to have the same amount as Tom!

Now, just because you don't have a full retirement plan in place yet, it doesn't mean you haven't been preparing in some manner. Many people we meet with have piles of money like 401(k)s, IRAs, stock portfolios, etc. Often these are part of your compensation package at work and are deducted from your paycheck. It's not uncommon for people to lose track of these types of assets. They don't open their statements, so they're out of sight and out of mind. We recommend you always read your account statements!

The key is to know what you have and how you can use it to reach your retirement goals. Also, if your employer contributes to your 401(k), we suggest you contribute up to their max amount, so you make the most out of this asset during your working years.

THE LATEST STRATEGIES

For most people, pensions are a relic of the past. The popular strategy of buying and holding stocks until you're ready to retire is also woefully outdated. It just doesn't account for today's volatile marketplace. New ways to build wealth are needed. That's where bucket planning comes into play.

Bucket planning is a strategy that works with **your** money. It is not a cookie-cutter product that a broker will try to sell you. It helps you organize your assets into a structure that can help hedge against market volatility and give you a reliable stream of income for your retirement. While one bucket is used to provide you with a stream of income, the others are filled based on their given investment strategies. Every bucket has a purpose. One is for income, while another is geared for growth, while another is for more speculative purposes. When one bucket is empty, you can dip into the next while the former replenishes itself. Keep in mind that each bucket fills with income that can be taxed differently and at different times.

The first bucket is filled with your ordinary work income, Social Security benefit, or stocks and is subject to taxation. The next bucket is made up of assets that are tax-deferred like your 401(k) or IRA. Meaning you pay taxes on them when you access them later in life. Then there's a bucket that's tax-free when you use it as income. Taxes were paid on these when you put money in. These assets generally include life insurance benefits, cash value life insurance, and Roth IRAs.

DISTRIBUTION

Distribution is when you move into the house. Distribution is your retirement! Like a well-crafted home built with quality materials, it is durable and designed to keep you comfortable. Like any home, there will be some routine maintenance, so you do have to work with your financial services provider on an ongoing basis. You don't want to find yourself using the furniture for firewood because the furnace has broken down!

Not only is this the next phase of your life, it is also the next phase in your complete retirement plan. There are new things to consider and strategies to employ. By working with your financial services provider on an ongoing basis, you can seamlessly move between these two phases.

For example, now that you're done working, it may be time to reconsider your 401(k) since your employer is no longer contributing. Know your options for withdrawing by contacting your 401(k)'s custodian. There may be age-based withdrawal rules or the possibility of transferring your money into an IRA. Like any investment, you need to be aware of all the fees that are involved as they could affect your strategy. Remember, there isn't just one way to do things. Know your options and go with the ones that best suit you and your goals in retirement. That can be different things to different people.

When you're in retirement, protecting your capital is critical. By carefully strategizing what asset to use and when to use it, you can fund your retirement without exhausting any of your accounts. This involves when to file for Social Security benefits, and how to take advantage of long-term growth vehicles like annuities. You can also use various forms of life insurance to not only leave something for your family but to generate income for yourself while you are alive. Taxes also play a critical role. An asset that looks like it could fund a good portion of your retirement can be drastically reduced by taxes. If it's not accessed at the right time or appropriately structured, you could be on the hook for a hefty bill.

Software can help you run scenarios for how all of these different assets can work together for your benefit. But software doesn't account for the human element the way actual humans can. You may be retired, but that doesn't mean you can't shift your priorities if things change. That's why you need to keep working with a professional. They can hear you out and make recommendations based on what you want, aside from strictly financial considerations. Diligence is required. With planning and partnership, you can enjoy the retirement you worked so hard for.

CHAPTER RECAP

- The sooner you start saving, the better.
- Maximize your 401(k)-employer contribution and know your withdrawal options.
- Bucket planning is a system to generate ongoing income for your retirement.
- Upon retirement, work with your financial services provider to revisit your strategy for various assets.

4

TAXES: "BUILDING PERMITS"

You already know that taxes are unavoidable. However, you'd be surprised how often people overlook them as they plan their retirement. It's like pulling permits to build a house. You've poured the foundation and have started building the frame, and all of a sudden, someone from the city shows up and gives you a big unexpected fine. Or, they shut you down altogether! Similarly, taxes, if not accounted for, can cause unexpected delays or potentially derail your retirement plans.

Tax planning as part of retirement planning is critical. It's one of the main components of a complete financial plan and can be your most significant expense in retirement. People think that their mortgage or student loans are their biggest expenses. Like other aspects of their finances, they can lose sight of an aspect that will play a huge role in how and when they retire. Every situation is different, but a plan needs to be in place. Even if you have an amount of money that makes you feel comfortable, it doesn't necessarily mean you can "afford" to pay a large amount of taxes. Determining your income after taxes is crucial as it affects when you can retire and whether your retirement will be what you imagine it to be.

Here are some things to be aware of when tax planning for retirement:

- Taxes on regular income sources.
- CD and mutual fund taxes.
- When do you pay taxes on an IRA?
- Tax implications from selling your business or home.
- The estate tax for very wealthy individuals.

New tax laws have also changed the calculus for many Americans, especially retirees. Deductions, tax brackets, and numerous other rules and regulations have changed. You need to consider whether itemization is as beneficial as claiming the new, larger standard deduction. These changes could also lessen the sting of Required Minimum Distributions (RMDs) from your IRA, as could a strategic roll out over time. Also, the cost of property taxes needs to be taken into consideration when deciding whether you should stay where you currently live, or if you should move when you retire. Medical expenses can play a role in your overall tax picture, as well.

Working with your financial services provider, you can help minimize the taxes you pay. Doing so can increase your income and your net worth. Tax diversification through bucket planning can help with this.

If you pay too much tax on an account, you run the risk of damaging your principal. If that happens, the account may never be healthy enough to draw income from again. Depending on your tax rate, certain investments also become more advantageous.

THE HIGHER THE TAX RATE, THE MORE ATTRACTIVE MUNICIPAL BONDS BECOME				
REGULAR FEDERAL TAX EXEMPT YIELD (%)	3.0	4.0	5.0	6.0
FEDERAL TAX RATE (%)	TAXABLE EQUIVALENT YIELD (%)			
10	3.3	4.4	5.6	6.7
15	3.5	4.7	5.9	7.1
22	3.8	5.1	6.4	7.7
24	3.9	5.3	6.6	7.9
32	4.4	5.9	7.4	8.8
35	4.6	6.2	7.7	9.2

Here's a scenario to illustrate the point. A retired couple in the 25 percent tax bracket lives on Social Security benefits and investment income. Municipal bonds make up most of their investments and enjoy a yield of 6 percent. The equivalent yield from a taxable investment would have to be 8 percent. That's a big difference. Municipal bond interest is taxed on their Social Security at 21.25 percent. That means the yield on their municipal bonds is now 4.725 percent. That makes the taxable equivalent yield 6.3 percent, which is a smaller gap of 1.575 percent.

Tax laws and regulations can change one way or the other. But, it's prudent to prepare for paying higher taxes. As government debt levels rise ever higher, the pressure to address the issue becomes even more significant. Cutting entitlements is another avenue for addressing rising debt, but that will affect millions of people—especially retirees. Inflation could also increase, devaluing the money you already have if the government prints more money to pay debts.

CHAPTER RECAP

- Tax planning is just as important as other parts of a complete retirement plan.
- Paying too much in taxes can permanently damage an investment account.
- Build a diversified portfolio.
- Consider converting your IRA to a Roth IRA to create a source of tax-free income.

5
RISK AND ASSET CATEGORIZATION

Having a well thought out strategy for every part of your retirement is essential, and this chapter covers two parts of the planning process that drive that point home. Assessing your tolerance for risk and organizing your assets requires expertise and experience. While you're in charge of the process, working with a financial services provider and their team allows you to tap their skills for your benefit. This is another example of how doing everything yourself can possibly be very detrimental to your financial future. If you hire a roofer, do you climb up the ladder and grab the nail gun from one of the worker's hands and start nailing in shingles? Of course not! You're talking to the job foreman down on the lawn. Before the work even begins, you've agreed upon what materials to use, how long the job will take, and how much it will cost. Their expertise and experience will guide you towards making more informed decisions.

RISK

Whether you have a lot or a little, everyone has a threshold for risk that they're not willing to cross. Many individuals don't realize how much risk their assets are actually exposed to. Furthermore, many brokers won't take the time to explain this to you. They're just selling you a product and not considering your best interests.

We like to begin by getting to know our clients and asking them how they would feel in certain situations to gauge their appetite for risk.

RISK VS RETURN TRADE-OFF

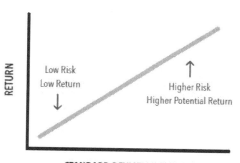

Say you're about to head out to dinner with friends on a Friday night. On the way out the door, you remember that you haven't checked the mail and stop for a moment to grab it. There, on the top of the stack, is a statement for your 401(k) or another account. Opening it can wait, but at that moment, you instinctually open it up to see what's inside. The news is not good. Your

$100,000 has withered to $80,000. Now what? How does that make you feel?

Have you suddenly lost your appetite, and is the weekend ruined? Are you likely to call us first thing on Monday morning to vent, or are you someone who believes that markets go up and markets go down? Are you confident in your plan and able to enjoy your weekend? There's no right or wrong answer to that. Planning for retirement isn't just about making the most money. You also have to be comfortable and enjoy your life.

By determining your threshold for risk and seeing how exposed your current assets are, the process of tailoring a plan gets easier. You'll feel freer to have additional conversations so we can determine how much money you need to protect for guaranteed income and how to position your other assets for growth and other financial goals beyond income.

THE RULE OF 100

The Rule Of 100 has been broadly used to help individuals determine their tolerance for risk. It helped people understand how their assets should be allocated based on their age. If you're younger, you can invest in assets that carry more risk since you still have time to recover from market volatility. If you're older, the assets you have should be more risk-averse since you are closer to, or are in retirement.

While this rule has generally served people well over the years, it no longer accounts for the increasing complexity and new challenges facing prospective retirees today. It's like trying to use all of today's modern tech gadgets with a dial-up Internet connection from the 1990s. The bandwidth of the connection can't even come close to supplying a new tablet or smartphone with the data it needs to perform up to its full potential. Instead of using all of the latest features and functions, your state-of-the-art machine is hamstrung. In this way, the Rule Of 100 doesn't have the bandwidth to take your personality, emotions, or goals outside of dollars and cents into account. Without incorporating those things into your retirement equation, the math won't work out the way you want it to.

ASSET CATEGORIZATION

This is what we like to consider the architectural phase of a retirement plan. It is the part where we meet and draw up your plan like a set of blueprints. Then, based on what you like or don't like, we make new drafts until you're happy. The following graph is a helpful visual for quickly determining the different categories your assets fall into.

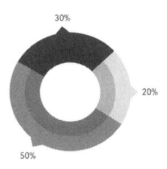

The 30 percent portion is green money and that is the base of your retirement income. It is money that has a low exposure to risk but will generally not generate eye-popping returns either. By planning for efficient distribution, you can maximize gains from this money. Bank accounts, different types of annuities, and indexed universal life insurance are all examples of this type of money.

The yellow 20 percent portion is money that is at some risk but has more potential for growth. Generally, a professional is managing this portion and using tools like advanced software to dispassionately keep this asset growing. It shields you from the personal pressure that these types of investments generate while allowing you to still enjoy their substantial upside.

Finally, the red 50 percent portion is, as you probably guessed, at the most risk. It has the highest upside, as well. Once you have built up a reliable stream of income, you can make investments of this type. Variable life insurance, Exchange Trade Funds (ETFs), stocks, and private equity all fall into this category.

TECHNOLOGY

Having a productive conversation, coming to understand your tolerance for risk, and categorizing your assets are essential. As in most other aspects of life, technology can play a role in facilitating this discussion. Your financial services provider can run simulations of financial scenarios. By running them based on various levels of risk, you can gauge your comfort level and view your assets by category quickly and efficiently. It could help you think of things in a new way or discover feelings on the subject that you didn't know you had. Writing things down on paper can make some people feel like they're on the spot, even if they are comfortable having a candid conversation. It's an example of using technology to aid in and not replace a well-crafted retirement plan. It's a powerful one-two punch.

In the end, you should have a clear understanding of your feelings on these subjects. You should also know what assets you own and know their level of risk so you can move forward with a plan.

While it's not the risk we're talking about precisely in this chapter, technology can help you stay in compliance with government regulations. Like everything else these days, there are more rules and regulations than ever. Primarily, they are designed to protect individual investors and aid in transparency. Without automation and technology, it would almost be impossible to achieve this level of regulation and transparency. Think of how many packages UPS ships every day. Do you think without a high level of technology, they could sort, route, and send the number of boxes they do every day? We take it for granted that things will arrive when they say they will. Yet we still find ourselves using tracking numbers to follow our order's journey from the warehouse to our front step. In this way, technology can give us peace of mind and raise our expectations.

CHAPTER RECAP

- Discover or articulate your threshold for risk with your financial services provider.
- Know what assets you have and categorize them according to risk.
- You need more than just the Rule Of 100 to accurately determine your risk tolerance.
- Technology can help assess your tolerance for risk and help comply with government regulations.

6

SOCIAL SECURITY

Social Security is the bedrock of retirement for most Americans. Established in 1935 as part of the New Deal by President Franklin Roosevelt, the plan aimed to ensure older Americans had a minimum amount of income to cover necessary expenses. It is a continual topic of debate for politicians and everyday people as it affects almost every American in one way or another.

While some question if it can continue, we believe that as long as people are paying into it, there will still be a program.

There are indeed fewer young workers contributing to the system than there are seniors drawing money out. But the system is so deeply ingrained into our society and economy that it is highly unlikely the program will be going anywhere in our lifetimes. More likely is that the government will continue to modify the program around the edges. That may involve increasing the age at which you can retire and still claim your benefit without any sort of reduction. It will also probably include raising taxes.

On its own, Social Security is not a complete retirement plan. In the decades since it was established, the program has significantly changed in scope and complexity. Benefits have been made available to more than just the person that initially earned them. Their children, dependents, spouses, and even ex-spouses can potentially be eligible to receive them in some part.

The decision to file for Social Security is more complicated than you might think. There's more to think about than how fast you can get your money. Taxes and other benefits, including Medicare, Medicaid, and spousal benefits, should all be considered when you are thinking of accessing this resource. The amount you get in each check is determined by an equation that is partially based on your best 35 earning years. If you file, then realize it would have been better not to have done so, you can return the money within the first year. Doing so will let your benefits continue to grow. Like other aspects of your retirement plan, we can run maximization reports. They will cover every possible filing decision to ensure you're making the decision that's best for your unique set of circumstances.

One of the biggest mistakes we see people make is not understanding what their Full Retirement Age (FRA) is. Depending on when you were born, it's either age 66 or 67. Generally, the longer you wait to draw from Social Security, the more you will receive per monthly check. You'll receive the highest dollar amount by waiting till the age of 70. As you can see in the next chart, the difference in the amount from age 62 to age 70 is significant in both the monthly and lifetime benefit amounts. Waiting until the age of 70 to file can also maximize the value of your benefit that your spouse could receive if you pass away before them.

AGE	MONTHLY BENEFIT	LIFETIME BENEFIT*
62	$994	$326,841
63	$1,078	$335,870
64	$1,186	$349,772
65	$1,296	$361,321
66	$1,410	$370,444
67	$1545	$381,696
68	$1,684	$389,948
69	$1,828	$395,128
70	$1,975	$397,192

Getting the most out of this asset can put less pressure on your other assets and help you bridge the income gap. The income gap is the difference between what you're projected to receive during retirement versus what your expenses will be. If you experience a gap in your income, it could force you to access an account too early or draw it down too low, both of which could prevent you from getting the most out of that specific account. You could also be setting yourself up to pay more taxes on your IRA and Social Security income. As with other parts of your retirement plan, your financial services provider will be able to help you find solutions to this challenge.

It is worth mentioning that waiting to take your benefit isn't always a silver bullet solution to Social Security election. It may or may not be the best choice depending on your situation. If it is not going to be your primary source of income, then you might not be concerned when you file and might be comfortable accessing it at age 62. You also might have a medical condition and the most prudent course of action is to file sooner rather than later.

Once you have filed for benefits, you do still have the option of continuing to work. Whether it is strictly to bolster your income, or you just love what you do, there are additional tax considerations to take into account. If you do file before your FRA and make more than the Social Security earnings limit for that year, you'll face higher taxation on any income above that amount. This consideration falls away once you do reach your FRA.

THE PROCESS

While you pay into the system with dollars and cents, as you can see on your W-2 form, your eligibility is based on credits. You need at least 40 credits to begin drawing benefits. Each credit equals a fixed amount of time that you have been paying into the system, which brings up an important point. While it may casually be called an entitlement program, the reality is you are merely tapping the income that *you* contributed to the system. Your benefits are the result of a lot of hard work that you put in.

You may think that accessing your benefits will be difficult since you'll be working with a large government agency. The good news is that you are now able to apply for your benefits online and spare yourself the inconvenience of trying to schedule an office visit months in advance. Employees of the Social Security Administration are barred from helping you with regard to your application strategy. However, the speed of accessing your benefits makes retirement planning all that much easier, and it allows you to have the most precise picture possible of your situation as you work with your financial services provider.

CHAPTER RECAP

- Work with your financial services provider to determine when you should file for your Social Security benefits.
- Despite all of the rhetoric, it is doubtful the Social Security program will be going anywhere in our lifetimes.
- Knowing your Full Retirement Age (FRA) is critical.
- Maximizing this asset helps your other assets reach their full potential.
- Social Security alone is not a comprehensive retirement plan.

7

BUILT TO LAST

We've said it once; we'll say it again. YOYO! *You're on your own* in building income that will last throughout your retirement and beyond, if you intend to leave a legacy. As funding employee retirement became an overwhelming task for companies, defined-contribution plans like 401(k)s became the standard. The Baby Boomers are the first generation where this is the norm; so, while this has been going on for decades, it is still a new phenomenon. Together with your financial service professional, you can meet the challenge this reality poses.

The starting point is determining a dollar amount that can maintain your lifestyle. People worry that process can be unduly complicated, but we trust that you know what your expenses are and start with that number. That's the net amount of money needed. From there, we can work backward to develop a plan to get to that figure.

OTHER FINANCIAL CONSIDERATIONS

Ensuring you have enough funds to provide for your immediate expenses is the primary concern. Generally speaking, when developing an income strategy as part of a complete retirement plan, this is the primary goal. That's not the only concern, though. Providing for immediate and extended members of your family can also be something you need to address. Perhaps you have a family member who is disabled and requires special care or living arrangements. Maybe you have grown children who are experiencing financial hardship, and you would like to help provide some support to them and your grandchildren. If a member of your family goes through a divorce, their personal and financial situation will be upended. If it's your goal to help in any of these situations, we can help you look at your options and choose the one that makes the most sense.

POTENTIAL HAZARDS

Organizing, strategizing, and putting together a plan can only go so far if you are burdened with a heavy debt load. Developing and sticking to a budget is essential. We like to say that you have paychecks and *playchecks*. Paychecks are for income to cover your expenses and for filling buckets of income for the future. There can also be a fun bucket to generate playchecks! Use this money for things that aren't essential to meeting your needs. It can't be all work and no play! Having a stack of *funbucks* can make being responsible with the rest or your assets easier. Other hazards include:

- Inflation—Unforeseen government policy or other economic factors that reduce the buying power of your money.
- Taxes—Plan for them to rise over the long term.

- Long-term care—According to a survey, the cost can range from $45,000 to over $97,000 per year*.
- Health Insurance Gap—If you retire before your eligible for Medicare you need to have insurance to cover yourself in case something serious happens.

SAFE GROWTH

Your financial service professional understands that markets today behave entirely differently than they have in the past. Financial products, including annuities and cash value life insurance, are options to help you grow your assets while not exposing yourself to risk.

LIFE INSURANCE

It's an option for providing for your spouse or other family members. We've all heard of it, and it's a product that has been around for a long time. Whether it's on the side of a blimp floating above a stadium, on a billboard, or aired on various TV or radio commercials, chances are you're familiar with a few of the big players in this industry.

We perform a life insurance review to see what policies you already have and how we can improve them. Often, we can do a strategic rollout in conjunction with your IRA. If you are over 59 ½ years old, you can make withdrawals from your IRA to fund a cash value life insurance policy. It can reduce the taxes on your IRA over time, and you get to avoid the 10 percent early withdrawal penalty. It's a way to avoid paying unnecessary taxes on one product while building another that can also be tapped later on, tax-free!

Cash value life insurance is one option that many wealthy individuals use, though many other people can benefit from it as

---

* *https://www.genworth.com/aging-and-you/finances/cost-of-care.html*

well. Designed in the right way, it can provide more benefits than you might think and offer a nice tax-free reward in the future. It can help keep money in your family, provide for tax-free income, and provide long-term care benefits.

Choosing the right provider is also essential. We look for companies whose main focus is life insurance. Providing policies should be their bread and butter, not an additional service they happen to offer. By factoring in your age, the amount you want to contribute, premium amount, and other factors, we can find the best company and form of life insurance for you. Your goals and circumstances can also affect the amount and type you buy. The death benefit can be the primary consideration if you're using it to care for others after you're gone. If you are using it for income planning or retirement, you can buy a policy with more living benefits.

If you own a business, passing it down to your children can be a worthwhile goal. But if not all your children are interested in taking it over, life insurance is an option for passing something down to them as well. This process is known as estate equalization. Let's say you own a restaurant, have two kids, and would like to pass the company on to them someday. The years go by, and your kids grow up. One of them moves away to pursue another career. The other loves the restaurant business and has made it their full-time job. You love your kids equally and want to provide something for both of them. What do you do? You could try to save money that is equivalent to the second child's share of the business, but that's decades of continual saving and might not be a realistic option. The child who wants to keep the company could also borrow the money to buy it from you. But that would saddle them with a heavy debt load and wouldn't set them up for success. Plus, you want to leave them with something, not sell them something! Purchasing a life insurance policy and designating the child who is uninvolved in the business as the beneficiary can be a solution to this dilemma. It allows you to leave something for them and pass the restaurant to your child who wants it.

Like saving money or investing, the earlier you buy life insurance, the better. The younger you are when you enter into a policy, the lower your premiums will be. The healthier you are the better, as well.

ANNUITIES

Annuities, just like any financial products, are neither good nor bad. There are good and bad options depending on your goals and situation. They are designed to provide you with income based on the amount of money you put into an insurance policy. They can provide you with growth without experiencing loss*, which is a great thing. Ensure you select the right one by working with your financial services provider. This type of annuity could be great for one of your financial buckets but ill-suited for bucket two, three or four, etc.

TYPES OF ANNUITIES

Here is a summary of different types of annuities. They all have pros, cons, and differences in how they work.

If your primary objective is growth, then the variable annuity could be an option. You get the flexibility to access several different investments at once with a single product. The growth is tax-deferred. But you are exposed to risk depending on how these investments perform and depending on market volatility.

Like a fixed annuity, fixed index annuities (FIAs) start by giving an insurance company a set amount of money upfront. In return, they provide you with interest on that amount. What separates the FIAs from their more-traditional counterparts is that

---

* All guarantees are backed by the claims paying ability of the insurer.

your interest rate is based on the performance of a given index, like the S&P 500 or NASDAQ, for example.

To start drawing payments from your annuity in a shorter time frame, the single-premium immediate annuity (SPIA) is an option. SPIAs begin by paying a lump sum to your insurance company. They may not come with some of the other benefits other options have, but you're able to turn it into a form of income much faster. That makes this form of annuity attractive to people in certain situations.

ANNUITY BENEFITS	VARIABLE ANNUITY	MULTI YEAR GUARANTEED ANNUITY	FIXED INDEXED ANNUITY	SINGLE PREMIUM IMMEDIATE ANNUITY
Offers a choice of how you receive income, including guaranteed income for life	✓		✓	✓
Offers the potential to grow your assets through a selection of investment options	✓			
Grows your assets at a fixed rate of return		✓		
Provides asset growth potential based on performance of a market index, such as the Standard & Poor's® 500			✓	
Guarantees your account value will never go down due to market volatility		✓	✓	
Can provide protection from market volatility through optional benefits	✓			
Provides a steady, guaranteed stream of income immediately after you purchase it				✓
All growth within the annuity compounds tax-deferred	✓	✓	✓	
Provides a financial legacy for your beneficiaries*	✓	✓	✓	*

Another type of deferred fixed annuity is the multi-year guaranteed annuity (MYGA). You'll receive a fixed rate of return over a set amount of time after paying a lump sum.

If you think an FIA might be an option, discuss it with your financial services provider. They'll go over every aspect of this type of investment, including something called the annual reset.

Annual reset allows you to keep the value of your annuity going up without fear of it going down. However, these gains are capped at a preset amount. Any increase past that amount goes to the insurance company. The trade-off is that they bare the brunt of any losses while your annuity remains untouched. It is an attractive feature for many retirees.

As you can see in the chart below, the value of your annuity climbs higher in a methodical manner. The market index, on the other hand, as represented by the dotted line, takes a severe drop from year two to year three. It rallies somewhat from year three to four but did not fully recover.

POWER OF ANNUAL RESET

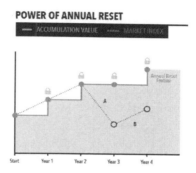

This chart is for informational purposes only and is not intended to be a projection or prediction of current or future performance of any specific product. All financial products have an element of risk and may experience loss. Past performance is not indicative of future results.

This type of investment is generally geared for the long haul and can be used to fill your income gap. The assumption with this type of product is that over extended periods, the market will go up. As the name implies, its value is measured yearly based on when you purchase it.

SEQUENCE OF RETURNS

To illustrate how important it is to protect your income during retirement, you can look to a phenomenon known as the *sequence of returns*. During the distribution phase, market volatility will be top of mind. That's different than in the accumulation phase of life, especially at the beginning of retirement when it can be tough to stomach significant market losses. Losses later in retirement are more manageable, as you have had time to realize some gains. Your assets may only partially fund your retirement if they are not appropriately managed by considering risk tolerance; that is if they can provide any funds at all.

In the following chart you can see two portfolios side by side. They start with the same amount and end with the same amount, but from year to year, they behave very differently. Portfolio A is outpacing Portfolio B by a considerable margin at year 10, but as time rolls on, things change. By year 20, Portfolio A has leveled off, and Portfolio B has rallied back from where it was at the midway point to pull even with its counterpart.

That's great when you're considering yearly averages during the accumulation stage. It really doesn't matter how you get to the number you need. It just matters that you get there. However, when you have retired and are in the distribution stage, this same scenario can be disastrous. When you're retired, you're tapping assets for income. You know what your expenses are, and you need to draw a specific dollar amount out to meet them. The timing of these withdrawals can have a massive impact on your assets. If you withdraw a fixed amount and don't account for downturns in the market, it becomes harder and harder to recover the losses. The gains to get back to even will need to be

$500,000 PURPOSE: ACCUMULATION

YEAR	PORTFOLIO A RETURN	PORTFOLIO A VALUE	PORTFOLIO B RETURN	PORTFOLIO B VALUE
0		500,000		500,000
1	33%	665,000	-28%	360,000
2	-5%	631,750	-3%	360,000
3	32%	833,910	16%	412,056
4	6%	833,910	-2%	403,815
5	12%	996,018	13%	456,311
6	-2%	970,218	27%	579,515
7	36%	1,319,496	-24%	440,431
8	21%	1,396,590	-8%	405,197
9	34%	2,139,431	-12%	356,573
10	37%	2,921,020	23%	438,585
11	23%	3,605,155	37%	600,861
12	-12%	3,172,536	34%	805,154
13	-8%	2,918,733	21%	974,237
14	-24%	2,218,237	36%	1,324,962
15	27%	2,817,161	-2%	1,298,462
16	13%	3,182,392	12%	1,454,278
17	-2%	3,119,724	6%	1,541,535
18	18%	3,119,724	32%	2,034,826
19	-8%	3,119,724	-5%	1,933,084
20	-28%	2,571,002	33%	2,571,002
AVERAGE ANNUAL RATE OF RETURN	10.4%		10.4%	

even higher. That can be difficult, if not impossible, to achieve if you let things deteriorate too far. The next chart demonstrates this point.

Like the previous chart, the average annual rate of return is the same. The difference is now you are relying on this asset for yearly withdrawals. The plan is to take five percent out annually, which is $25,000. Assuming you are gaining at least that much each year, this shouldn't be a problem. You are merely living off the gains while the principal remains there for future growth.

The problem is, the market doesn't just go up, up, and up. If you continue to take $25,000 out even in market downturns, you can see how things begin to fall apart. You are not taking out just five percent. That $25,000 becomes a bigger and bigger percentage of the overall total as your principal shrinks. The individual with Portfolio B didn't work with their financial services provider to develop a complete plan! They were using the wrong bucket for income; or, it was their only bucket!

Asset distribution is critical. You need to protect the money you rely on for steady income from risk. Use other assets that are more exposed to risk for immediate sources of income. They should be allowed to grow, and at the right time you can access these funds with a coordinated and well thought out bucket strategy.

$500,000 PURPOSE: INCOME
$25,000 annual withdrawal, 3% annual increase

YEAR	PORTFOLIO A		PORTFOLIO B	
	RETURN	VALUE	RETURN	VALUE
0		$500,000		$500,000
1	33	635,875	28%	338,500
2	-5	578,975	3%	307,981
3	32	733,481	18%	328,668
4	6	749,352	-2%	294,991
5	12	809,448	13%	303,273
6	-2	764,587	22%	352,390
7	38	1,004,587	-24%	241,547
8	21	1,181,375	-8%	192,708
9	34	1,546,257	-12%	139,812
10	37	2,029,739	23%	138,599
11	23	2,520,592	37%	145,957
12	-12	2,165,592	34%	155,093
13	-4	1,976,526	21%	148,278
14	-24	1,469,852	38%	158,334
15	27	1,823,793	-2%	117,731
16	13	2,019,405	12%	98,572
17	2	1,939,300	6%	54,685
18	14	2,142,334	32%	24,212
19	-3	2,184,112	-5%	0
20	-25	1,498,660	33%	0
AVERAGE ANNUAL RATE OF RETURN				
	10.4%		10.4%	

CHAPTER RECAP

- The Baby Boomer generation is the first generation to deal with defined-contribution plans.
- Work backward from the net dollar amount you need to maintain your current lifestyle and develop a plan on how to reach that figure.
- There are options available to provide for children and grandchildren, while also ensuring you have income for your retirement.
- Life insurance can provide legacy benefits for your spouse and extended family, but can also be an option for income during retirement.
- Annuities can provide another stream of long-term income.
- Educate yourself about the various types to determine which one, if any, is right for you.
- The money you rely on for income should be protected from risk as much as possible!

8
LEGACY

You have achieved this much in life by educating yourself, working hard, and just generally being a responsible and hardworking person. When your time comes, wouldn't you like to be remembered for these qualities? Many people will remember you for just those things. But without proper planning, your estate and assets can appear unorganized and your wishes a mystery to even your family and friends. It can cause unintentional strife and add an undue burden to those who are grieving and dealing with funeral arrangements and myriad other issues.

A legacy can mean whatever you want it to mean. Often the term is only associated with very wealthy individuals. Think of the Ford and Rockefeller foundations. But that's not true. It can be as simple as ensuring a family heirloom is handed down through the generations, or as big as ensuring that you transfer the family farm to your children. You don't even have to pass anything on.

Ensuring your bills are paid and everything is accounted for can be a massive gift on its own.

It is your opportunity to ensure that your wishes are followed, and a chance to look after your family, friends, or organizations one last time. Planning can encompass the distribution of assets, both financial and material, along with the distribution of life insurance death benefits. It is YOUR legacy. How do you want to handle it? Work with your financial services provider to ensure any plan speaks for you and not for someone else.

LIVING TRUSTS	WILLS
Avoids Probate	Probate Required
Private	Public
Incapacity Management	Effective at Death Only

Details matter. Often we meet with widows or widowers who are dealing with estate issues and wish their spouse had done some planning ahead of time. By ensuring beneficiaries are in place and that all of the appropriate documents and forms are filled out fully and accurately, you can make things much more manageable. It's not that expensive to get your affairs in order as part of a complete retirement plan. However, it can be costly for your family to handle after the fact. If your family is unable to handle things, it can fall to the courts through the public process of probate.

As you can see in the previous graph, even if you have a will, probate will be part of the process. Living trusts are another option and give more control and the ability to avoid probate. Remember, your financial services provider is there for you. They can handle all of the fine details to ensure the process is as smooth as possible and to avoid adding stress to an already stressful time.

Here are some of the main strategies we employ for legacy planning:

- IRA Distribution Planning
- Secure Act Planning
- Charitable donations.
- Leveraging your assets using life insurance.
- Creating a family trust or foundation.
- Establishing a donor-advised fund.
- Using a charitable remainder annuity trust.

Congress just passed major retirement law changes, and it could impact your retirement income or the legacy you hope to leave your beneficiaries. New provisions affect required minimum distributions, IRA options, and potentially when you can access your pension plan dollars. It also may present new opportunities for you to create an income stream that you won't outlive.

Contact MaggiTax Advisory & Financial Group, LLC or visit our website at www.maggitax.com or call 833-Maggitax.com and see how these changes could affect you. They became law on January 1, 2020 so don't delay.

Earlier, we talked about life insurance and how you can use RMDs to fund policies for a tax-free asset you can leave behind. Depending on your date of birth, you are required to start withdrawing from your IRA or pay hefty penalties. If you obtained age 70.5 by 12/31/2019, your first distribution is required to take place for 2019. If you obtained age 70.5 on 1/1/2020 or later, you have until age 72 to begin taking RMD's. You have the ability to delay taking your first RMD until April 1st of the following year, however 2 distributions will then be required for that year. You can also use RMDs for charitable giving or further investing.

USING RMDS WITH LIFE INSURANCE

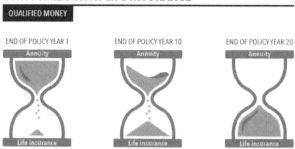

CHAPTER RECAP

- A plan has to be in place for your final wishes to be followed.
- Details matter—ensure documents and forms are thoroughly and accurately filled out.
- It can be expensive and frustrating for your spouse and family to sort through your estate once you're gone, and there isn't a plan.
- It falls to the government to handle your estate if no one else will.
- RMDs from your IRA can fund future tax-free benefits in the form of life insurance.

9
STAY IN TOUCH LEGACY

Now that you've developed a plan or are already retired, it is essential to keep the lines of communication between you and your financial services provider open. Markets change, situations change, people change! You need to stay on top of the latest trends and keep track of your assets to ensure you're getting the most out of them.

A bonus of working with a professional on an ongoing basis is that they can monitor your accounts for you while you live your life. If they see something that's not right or something on the horizon, they can be a proactive partner and look out for your best interests, allowing you to spend more time with your family, and pursuing your passions.

It's normal to make changes to your plan as you go along, so don't feel like you have done something wrong if you need to update things. Unexpected events, whether they're welcome or unwelcome, can cause you to shift your priorities. You may want to add beneficiaries to specific assets. You also may want to add beneficiaries to *new* assets. New products come up from time to time, and while you certainly shouldn't be buying everything that comes down the pike, it never hurts to see what's new. If, after a consultation, you decide that you're comfortable with a new product and it makes sense for your situation, you can add it to your portfolio. Paying off a mortgage, student loans, or other large debts are also causes for reassessing your portfolio. It could be a chance to funnel extra cash into buckets for future growth or to bolster your income for immediate needs.

Technology has made it easier than ever to stay in touch and up to date. We can run additional reports and simulations if your situation changes drastically, and it can make decision making more precise. It can also aid in keeping all of your records organized and secure. Formulating your plan takes more than just dollars and cents into consideration. The human element must also play a leading role. Once your plan has been put into action, technology can streamline its execution and help you quickly understand what's in front of you.

An added bonus is that you won't be as reliant on traditional paper mail. You'll also be able to cut down on trips to your financial services provider. While your financial services provider is keeping track of the latest trends and market fluctuations, you can use technology to do additional research yourself. It can help you ask better questions and be an engaged partner in your financial affairs. Be sure to visit our website at https://maggitax.com as well.

It is also good to keep security in mind when accessing sensitive information on your computer, tablet, or phone. It's hard to miss all of the news stories concerning confidential data compromised through different underhanded methods. Make sure to keep passwords and usernames private. Be sure you or your financial services provider are the only ones that can access any systems that store your account information.

We hope you have found this book useful and wish you the best as you prepare for and enjoy your retirement. Remember that a plan isn't merely just a piece of paper. A plan is really about education and putting that education into practice. Generating a complete plan is a process of learning what you have, and exploring options to arrive at your desired goals. No one can start over, but you can start right now!

CHAPTER RECAP

- Staying in contact with your financial services professional is essential to your retirement goals.
- Updating your plan based on new circumstances is normal.
- Technology can help in the decision-making process and reduce the amount of paper and physical records you need to store.
- Let your financial services provider handle the day to day work.
- Focus on your career or retirement!

Made in the USA
Columbia, SC
31 August 2021